Live your Dreams

Live your Dreams

by Ian Thorpe

A Scholastic Press book
from
Scholastic Australia

www.ianthorpe.telstra.com.au

Scholastic Press
345 Pacific Highway
Lindfield NSW 2070
An imprint of Scholastic Australia Pty Limited (ABN 11 000 614 577)
PO Box 579
Gosford NSW 2250
www.scholastic.com.au

Part of the Scholastic Group
Sydney ● Auckland ● New York ● Toronto ● London ● Mexico City
● New Delhi ● Hong Kong ● Buenos Aries ● Puerto Rico

First published in 2002
Text copyright © Ian Thorpe, 2002.

Photographs on cover courtesy of adidas, Omega Seamaster fashion shoot January 2002, and Andrew Gash, photographer, © 2002.

All rights reserved. No part of this publication may be reproduced or transmitted in any form or by any means, electronic or mechanical, including photocopying, recording, storage in an information retrieval system, or otherwise without the prior written permission of the publisher, unless specifically permitted under the Australian Copyright Act 1968 as amended.

National Library of Australia Cataloguing-in-publications entry
   Thorpe, Ian, 1982-.
   Live your dreams.
   ISBN 1 86504 529 2.
      1.Thorpe, Ian,1982-. 2. Success - Juvenile literature.
      3.Goal (Psychology) - Juvenile literature. 4. Swimmers - Australia - Biography.
      I. Title. (Series: Living legends (Sydney, N.S.W.)).
158.1

Typeset in Gill Sans.

Printed in Hong Kong through Pheonix Offset.

10 9 8 7 6 5 4 3 2 1   2 3 4 5 6 / 0

Dedication

To all the future champions of the world, no matter in what field—and to Barry and Hicksy.

Some people think that you have to be a genius to be a winner. And some people think you have to win to succeed. But I know that this isn't necessarily true.

I know from my own experience in the pool that you don't have to beat your competitors to feel like a winner. I know that you don't have to come first in the race to feel you have succeeded.

I also know that there are no secrets to success.

As you probably know, I am a swimmer. I race at the top international level. To all appearances, I swim in order to win the race. So it might seem strange when I say that coming first in a race actually isn't all that important to me.

According to my philosophy of life, winning doesn't mean coming first. And coming first isn't necessarily a sign of success.

On the other hand, I see winning and success as things that anyone can achieve.

It all depends on how you look at it.

I'm hoping that the story of my life so far will show you what I mean. I'm hoping that a glimpse into how I approach swimming, racing and winning will give you an insight into how you might approach your own life—and how you can discover that you too can be a success and a winner… on your own terms.

Ian Thorpe
2002

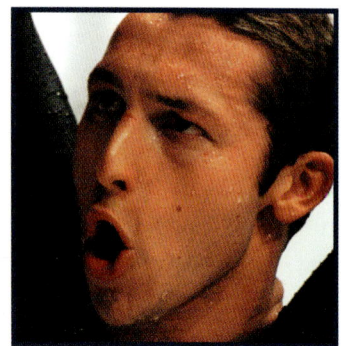

CONTENTS

The Wading Pool	10
First Strokes	14
The Hard Slog	20
Butterflies	26
The Finishing Line	28
Live Your Dreams	33
Living Your Life	38
Charity	42
Looking Ahead	45

THE WADING POOL

I had what would be considered a very normal upbringing. I grew up with my sister, Christina, who is nearly three years older than me. My father and mother both worked—my mum as a schoolteacher, and my dad as a council gardener. We lived in an average brick house in the ordinary garden suburbs of south-western Sydney, Australia, with a mowed lawn and a Hills Hoist clothes-line in the backyard.

"We lived in an average brick house in the ordinary garden suburbs of south-western Sydney..."

My sister and I did the same things as every other kid in the street. There were lots of playing fields and parks in the area, and some of my favorite memories are of playing down by the Georges River. I had a lot of friends, and on weekends we would do things together. We played soccer and ball games, but we did lots of mucking about, too—just being kids and running around in the bush. Playing Tarzan was a favourite, but although I loved swinging on vines, I was really bad at climbing trees. However, I loved building cubby houses, and the trampoline in our backyard made a perfect cubby frame. Cubby houses were big-time!

So was Lego. I was obsessively into Lego. Every time I went shopping with my parents, I always behaved extra well, just on the off-chance that I would be rewarded for my good behaviour with some new Lego. I would spend hours on it, following the directions in the diagrams, then destroying the model as soon as I'd finished building it, and starting on something more creative that I would make up myself.

"So was Lego. I was obsessively into Lego."

I went to a public school. I used to work very hard in class, whether I liked the subject or not. I saw everything that I did as a challenge—whether it was colouring in a picture or doing my spelling test. I'm still like that now. I love a challenge. I liked doing all sorts of different things. I liked art.

Did you know the first international prize I won was for art? It was a still-life painting of a vase with flowers and fruit. I guess my Year 4 teacher thought I showed some talent, and she entered my painting into an international competition. I wasn't even aware that someone had sent my painting overseas! I didn't know anything about it. I came second.

Painting, not drawing. I wasn't that good at the tiny details, but I was good at expressing an idea and giving an overall impression. I read a lot as well. The *Fudge* books were my favourites, and I used to read *Goosebumps*. I also used to read whatever my sister read. She was a bit older than I was, so that meant I was sometimes reading a bit further ahead than my friends. In one way that was good, but in another way it meant that I wasn't able to talk to my friends about the books I was enjoying.

I used to like cooking, too. I would help my nan, who was always making something—cakes, biscuits and things—which were unbelievably good. The cakes were meant to be iced, but we would take them out of the oven and eat them as soon as they were cool, so they never ended up getting their icing or their decorations. I still enjoy cooking, but now I cook proper meals.

Mum and Nan used to say I was a serious kid. They said I was serious about everything I did. If I was doing school work, it was serious business. If I was playing Lego, it was serious. Even now, people say my face looks really serious when I train. Maybe I'm a bit of a contradiction, because although on the outside I look so serious, on the inside I'm enjoying myself!

I probably look serious because I'm concentrating and being focused. I always want to get the best out of myself, to keep improving, to see what I can achieve next—so I tend to focus really hard.

Even when I played Lego, it wasn't enough just to follow the directions and make the model. I had to make my own thing, something bigger and better and more complicated, and beyond what I'd done before. Once the Lego house was finished, it was time to put on extensions!

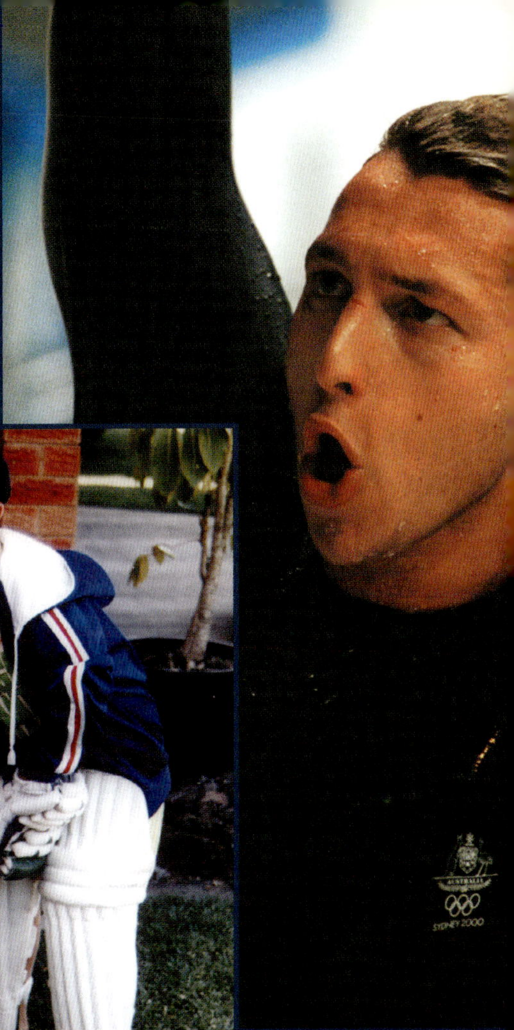

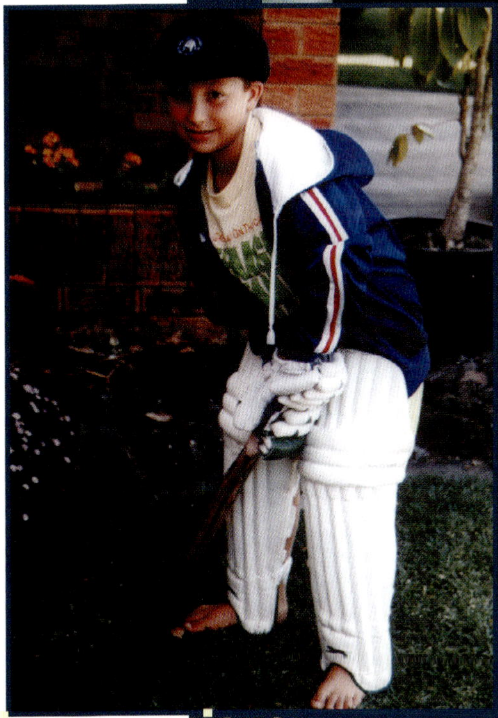

Although there are only four in my immediate family, the extended family is large. I have four cousins on my mum's side, and twelve on my dad's. We spent a lot of time together as we were growing up, and two or three families would often team up to go on holidays, to Forster especially, where we stayed in the caravan park. My cousins Paul and Michelle were with us most holidays, and I remember us playing pranks on our parents and generally having a silly, fun time. One memory of Forster was when Dad pushed us all off a raft and into the water. But there was only about ten centimetres of water, and under that there was thick mud. It was great, because we were always being told not to get dirty, and there we were, up to our armpits in mud for the rest of the day.

I was a serious kid. They said I was serious about everything I did.

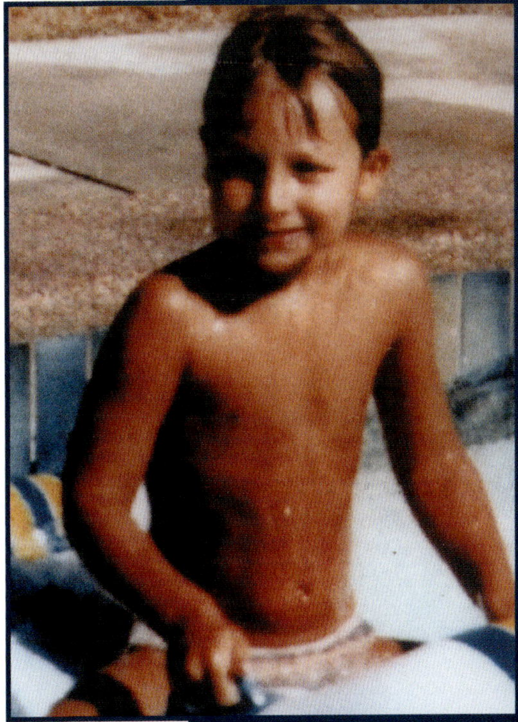

AUSTRALIAN SWIMMER OF THE YEAR

When I was young, I wanted to grow up to be so many different things. My ambitions changed from week to week. I wanted to be an architect one week, a physiotherapist the next, and a doctor the week after that. But never did I dream that I would end up being a swimmer!

"But I was allergic to chlori

Of course, like most kids, I learnt the basics of swimming when I was really young. But I was allergic to chlorine; I used to belly-flop into the pool and I swam with my head out of the water. In fact, in the beginning it was my sister who was the swimmer of the family. On Friday afternoons, Mum went with Christina to swimming training, while Dad took me to Little Athletics.

I played soccer, too, on Saturdays, while Christina played netball and swam in carnivals. I spent a lot of time going along to swimming carnivals and sitting and watching my sister swim, hour after hour. I used to get quite bored. There were some other people there that I went to school with,

FIRST STROKES

and when they started swimming, I thought to myself that if I had to be there, I might as well join in and start swimming too.

I was eight years old when I joined the swimming squad. I went to Padstow Pool, which was a twenty-five metre indoor pool. At first, squad was half an hour each week. It was mainly stroke correction, teaching me to drop my bad swimming habits and to develop the proper arm, leg and head movements. I soon got to the stage where I could enter the same competitions that my sister was swimming in, and my racing career began!

Meanwhile, I still kept up with soccer and Little Athletics. I loved it all, and by the time I was nine or ten, I only had one afternoon a week to myself. The weekends and every other afternoon were taken up with one thing or another. I never thought it was all too much, and tried to fit in everything else, as well as swimming.

I used to belly flop into the pool and I swam with my head out of the water

The first squad I was in was called 'Row Boats'. After a while, I went on to 'Tug Boats' and after that, 'Jet Boats'. When I got older, I went on to Pre-Seniors and Seniors.

But there came a time when I had to make a choice. Little Athletics and Swimming Club were on the same night, so I had to choose which one I was going to keep doing and which one I was going to drop. I guess I made the right decision!

I didn't start early morning training until later. My parents didn't push me to train hard at swimming when I was really young. I'm glad, because some kids are pushed by their parents or coaches to train too hard when they are young, and they can burn out quickly and give up swimming before they've got properly started. I began Saturday morning training when I was eleven. When I was twelve, I did Tuesday and Thursday morning training as well as Saturday morning and Friday night. It wasn't until I turned fourteen that I started doing ten swimming sessions a week.

Olympic Champion Titles

2000 Sydney—400m Freestyle
2000 Sydney—4 x 100m Freestyle Relay
2000 Sydney—4 x 200m Freestyle Relay

Swimming training means lots of time alone with your thoughts in the water. It gives you time to think about all sorts of things. When I first started swimming, I used to think of myself as a big cruise liner. In my mind, I made a machine out of my body. My heart was the engine, my brain was the battery, and whenever I had a drink of water, it was as if I was refuelling. I also had all these tiny little people inside me, powering and operating and working at different parts of the ship to help me go forward. If I needed to go faster, I would imagine the little people working harder and moving faster inside the ship. The whole ocean liner was controlled through my eyes, out of my goggles.

What I was doing in my imagination was turning something alive into a machine. When I turned my body into a machine like that, it helped take away the pain. It also made training that little bit more fun.

The year I turned fourteen, I had nearly all of winter off—almost two and a half months with no swimming at all. When I got back into training again, I started with five sessions a week, then built up to six, then eight, and then finally ten sessions of training a week.

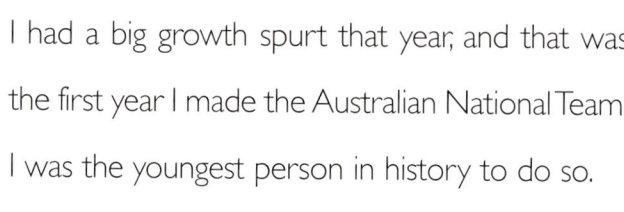

I had a big growth spurt that year, and that was the first year I made the Australian National Team. I was the youngest person in history to do so.

Even though people say I look serious when I train, I have never taken swimming seriously. I don't think it's right to take sport seriously. Sport is something we should enjoy. I've always enjoyed swimming, and if I stop enjoying it, I'll stop swimming, too.

One of the things I enjoy about sport, and especially about swimming, is all the things I have learnt. By that, I don't mean how to swim butterfly and freestyle—I mean what I have learnt about myself, and about life.

Sport is like a summary of life. What you put into it is what you get out of it.

The results of commitment to sport are so clear. If you commit yourself to your sport, you

will improve. It's as simple as that. And that's what life is all about, too. If you commit yourself to what you do, you will get so much more out of it. You'll feel satisfied with yourself. You'll feel self-fulfilled. This fulfillment can come through the experience itself, and not always the end result.

Swimming taught me that sport is not just about competing and winning. I have never been disappointed with what I achieve when I swim. This is because I always put as much effort as I possibly can into my training. So, whatever the result might be at the end of each race, no matter where I come in that race, I know that I have done the best that I possibly can—and that is very satisfying for me.

"Sport is not just about competing and winning. I have never been disappointed with what I achieve when I swim."

World Champion (long course) Titles

1998 Perth—400m Freestyle
1998 Perth—4 x 200m Freestyle Relay
2001 Japan—200m Freestyle
2001 Japan—400m Freestyle
2001 Japan—800m Freestyle
2001 Japan—4 x 100m Freestyle Relay
2001 Japan—4 x 100m Medley Relay
2001 Japan—4 x 200m Freestyle Relay

THE HARD SLOG

Most people only see the glamorous side of swimming—they see the thrill and excitement of competition and think that this is what being a swimmer is all about.

But competition is the aspect of swimming that takes up the least of my time. Most of my time is dedicated to hard work. Early morning starts. Four to five hours in the pool every day. Extra sessions of weight training, physiotherapy, yoga, boxing and massage. The strict diet. The thousands of kilometres that I swim every year.

"My day starts at 4.17 am. I get up and go to the pool for training for two to two and a half hours."

I first broke a world record in 1998. That was the year I turned 16.

My day starts at 4.17 am. I get up and go to the pool for two to two and a half hours of swimming training. Then I do weight training, and in the afternoons I do another two-hour swimming session. Between sessions I try to rest as much as I possibly can. Training is very tiring at times, so

you need to rest and give your body the opportunity to recover between sessions. I do this training program six days a week—just the same as everyone else in my squad.

Sample week of training

Day	Morning	Afternoon
Monday	arrive at pool 4.45am to **stretch** 2 – 2½ hours **swimming** from 5am 1 hour fitness session: **boxing**	2 – 2½ hours **swimming** from 4.30pm
Tuesday	arrive at pool 4.45am to **stretch** 2 – 2½ hours **swimming** from 5am 1 hour fitness session: **weights**	2 – 2½ hours **swimming** from 4.30pm
Wednesday	**sleep in** until 8.30am 1 hour fitness session: **boxing**	2 – 2½ hours **swimming** from 4.30pm
Thursday	arrive at pool 4.45am to **stretch** 2 – 2½ hours **swimming** from 5am 1 hour fitness session: **weights**	2 – 2½ hours **swimming** from 4.30pm
Friday	arrive at pool 4.45am to **stretch** 2 – 2½ hours **swimming** from 5am	2 – 2½ hours **swimming** from 4.30pm
Saturday	arrive at pool 5.15am to **stretch** 2 hours **swimming** 1 hour fitness session: **weights** 1 hour fitness session: **boxing**	
Sunday	day off	day off

I do boxing because, believe it or not, boxing uses the same muscle groups as swimming. My once-a-week massage is not one of those relaxing kinds of massages. It's actually quite painful. One of the most painful times is when the person massaging uses thumbs and elbows to dig deep into my muscles. It hurts, but it's important to have this weekly session because it helps to prevent injuries.

Even though the routine is the same each week, swimming training goes through different phases. These phases are tailored to the next competition. At the start of the season, there's an *aerobic build-up* phase that goes for three weeks, with a gradual increase in the number of kilometres I swim each day.

Then there's one week of *recovery*, with a little sprinting and fewer kilometres. Then follows three weeks of *endurance training* where I 'over-train', swimming lots of kilometres. It's a very intense phase. The most I have ever swum in an *endurance* phase was 127 kilometres in a week. That really hurt!

After *endurance training* there's a three-week *quality* phase. This is quite intense, too, with more focus on sprint work. Depending where I am in relation to the next competition,

I start again with the *endurance* phase, followed by the *quality* phase again.

Three weeks before a competition, I go into a *taper*. In this phase I drop the number of kilometres that I swim, and decrease the intensity of the training. This gives the muscles a chance to recover and develop before going into a competition. During the first week of a taper I'll swim fifty-five kilometres, in the second week I'll swim forty kilometres, and then thirty kilometres the week immediately before competing.

Training like this is physically demanding. I need plenty of rest, but on the mornings that I train, I never sleep in once the alarm has gone off. But on Wednesday and Sunday mornings, when there is no training, I sleep in until 8.30. Even so, I always set my alarm for 4.17 and let it go off at the usual time, so that I can have the luxury of switching it off and ignoring it! Two days a week, I have control over the clock, instead of the clock having control over me.

When we're in competition, however, I do sleep longer. I sleep until 7.30 every day of a competition. And I only do six to eight kilometres of swimming over the course of each day, just enough to maintain my fitness—although naturally I have to race on these days as well!

I've been lucky with my coach. I've had the same coach for the last ten years. He just happened to be the coach in the area where I lived, and where I learnt to swim. He has a series of successful swimming programs that he has developed out of his own 25-metre pool. In the swimming world, this is supposed to be impossible. Everyone says that you can't train successfully in a short-course pool. But my coach has trained four swimmers who made the Olympics, as well as a couple of swimmers who made the Commonwealth and National teams.

However, I now also have the luxury of swimming in a 50-metre outdoor pool, which is much more enjoyable.

BUTTERFLIES

When you compete in high-level sport such as international swimming, there can be a lot of people with certain expectations of you. If you look at these expectations in a negative way, they can turn into stress and pressure. But if you look at these expectations in a positive way, then they become support. You can use a situation either to your advantage, or to your disadvantage, depending on how you allow yourself to think.

When it comes time to compete, pressure and nerves can be either a good thing or a bad thing. If you feel nervous and sick in the stomach because you are worried about what other people expect of you, then you have nerves for the wrong reason.

Commonwealth Champion Titles

1998 Kuala Lumpur—200m Freestyle
1998 Kuala Lumpur—400m Freestyle
1998 Kuala Lumpur—4 x 100m Freestyle Relay
1998 Kuala Lumpur—4 x 200m Freestyle Relay

But if you have a strange feeling in your stomach because you really want to get in there and see how you can perform, then you have nerves for the right reason. When you know that you have done all your training, and you know that because of your preparation you are going to swim well, you can use this nervous energy to your advantage by getting out there and enjoying the opportunity. We have to enjoy competing, because we don't have that many opportunities to perform, and this is where all the hard work actually pays off.

I used to take the attitude that I should psyche myself up before a race, building up as much of that jittery, competitive energy as I could. Most people are taught that this is the best way to prepare. But it didn't work for me. It was the wrong attitude. It was unnatural for the kind of person I am. Psyching myself up created the wrong kind of nerves. It made me too stressed and too tense.

My whole philosophy now is to be relaxed. You use less energy and become more efficient in the water when you relax. I don't know how I do it, but I just … relax! One thing that helps, right before the race, is to try and think of anything but swimming. So I talk to my competitors; I chat. Another thing that helps is to recognise that I can't change my competitors' performances. They have done everything they possibly can to reach this stage, just as I have. There is nothing more to be done, so there's no point being concerned.

I race to enjoy myself, not to win. I've done the hard work and the preparation, so the race is where I enjoy the moment, and where I show myself what all the hard work was for.

"My whole philosophy now is to be relaxed. You use less energy and become more efficient in the water when you relax."

THE FINISHING LINE

When I was about sixteen, I was told that the most important thing I could do was win. I was racing in Brazil at the time, and was winning every event I entered. But I wasn't really making any extra effort. It is true, I was presenting a challenge to the other competitors—but I wasn't presenting a challenge to myself. And so, even though I was coming first, it wasn't really winning, and to me it wasn't fun.

 "I put so much effort into it, and was so exhausted after

You can come first by a centimetre, or by ten metres. I probably could have come first by ten metres that time in Brazil. But I didn't try. If I had tried, I would have felt more satisfied with my performance.

The whole thing is, I like to set my own standard, and then work towards achieving that. I compete against myself, not

against other people. That's how I get fulfillment from what I do. I can't affect what the other competitors are doing in the race. They are of no concern to me. But I do have control over what I do. So I give everything I've got, and then whatever the result, I'm happy. Winning is almost incidental.

In the Sydney 2000 Olympic 200-metre freestyle, I came second to Pieter van den Hoogenband. I actually thought I was going to swim faster that day. I put more preparation into that event than any other, and I put more effort into the race itself than into any other race. I put so much effort into it, and was so exhausted after it, that I struggled to get out of the pool. But when I touched the wall, I was happy.

I couldn't have put any more into that race. My main aim was to get out there and do my best. I'm the one who put in all those early mornings and all those hours of training. I expected myself to do my utmost, and because I did exactly that, I fulfilled my own expectations, and I was happy.

World Records—800m Freestyle

Hobart 26 March 2001—7:41.59
*Fukuoka 24 July 2001—7:39.16

* AT THE TIME OF WRITING, I STILL HOLD THIS RECORD

In my interpretation of winning and losing, I have never lost a race. That means that *you* can never lose a race, either. You are never beaten unless you accept that you have been beaten.

You can't change what other people are going to do. You can't control their performance. So there is no need to *worry* about what they're going to do, either. The best way to look at success is this: whatever you achieve, it is your own personal achievement. When you do something—whether you are in a team sport or an individual sport, whether it is at school or at home—if you know you have given it everything you possibly can, then you have won.

are going to do.
You can't control their performance.

It doesn't matter if you come first, second or last. It doesn't matter if you achieved more than you expected. It doesn't matter if you didn't achieve at the level you thought you could have achieved. What does matter is that if you know you have done your best, then you've won, no matter what.

In my life, I am my own greatest challenge. I am my own greatest challenger. Not Pieter van den Hoogenband, or Grant Hackett, or any other swimmer. I can't affect what they can do. I can only change what I can do. As far as I'm concerned, it is irrelevant whether they win or I win. It doesn't matter.

World Champion (short course) Titles

1999 Hong Kong—200m Freestyle
1999 Hong Kong—4 x 100m Freestyle Relay

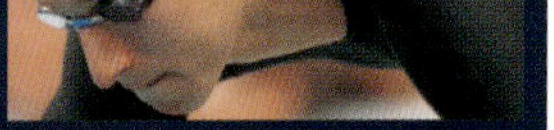

It is important to have a dream. And to achieve that dream, it is important to set goals. But sometimes the goals we set ourselves seem too huge and demanding. The goal seems so far away.

When I feel like this, I try to concentrate on something smaller. I look at trying to achieve small goals each day. I take segments out of the training session, and simply try to make it through to the next segment. I make that next segment my goal, rather than looking at the ultimate goal.

One step at a time, because distance can be daunting.

If I divide my main goal into smaller goals, by the end of the week I will have built a good foundation for moving towards a slightly bigger goal. Swimming is like building something—you have to have a foundation and a structure to work from when you are preparing for competition. Looking at the huge picture can overwhelm you, but looking at what you need to do today, or this week, is far easier. Making small contributions each day means that in a few days, a few weeks, a few months, or in a year, you will have reached the goal you once

LIVE YOUR DREAMS

thought was too far away. The work you do today gives you a good building block for tomorrow, and the block you build tomorrow supports the block you make the next day. If you work like this every day, the blocks you make will soon combine together to build a wall—and then you can add to the wall and build the building.

But sometimes it's the day-to-day work that seems too hard. That's when I look at the bigger picture again. I look at what I am trying to achieve. I try not to think about what is happening in the present, or the pain I am feeling at that moment, and instead try to think about how I am going to feel later on when I

am racing. I try to think of how proud I'll be of myself when I finally achieve my goals.

I always set my own goals. I believe it is extremely important to do this, and not set goals that other people want me to achieve. I don't worry about what other people expect of me. The goals I set are a very personal thing: I have my own expectations of myself, and they are what I try to fulfil.

But at the same time, it is important to have positive support from other people. I recognise that while I have been achieving things for myself, there have been many others who have contributed to my success. I am sure this applies to the successes in everyone's lives. Support can come from many places—from a coach, a relative, a friend or a teacher. They all support you in their own unique way.

I've been very lucky. My parents have supported me in many ways. For years, they took it in turns

to drive Christina and me to the pool every morning. They were so excited when Christina got her licence and took over the driving!

There is a kind of selfishness in getting all this support. I recognise that other people are giving up their own time to help me achieve my goals. But you need other people if you want to follow your dream to the highest level. It's good to remember that it is often other people's contributions that allow you your success.

Achievement and goal-setting are personal things. I like to challenge myself, so I set high standards. I know that with the right amount of focus, attention and dedication, I can achieve these high standards and turn them into a reality. If you set your own goals and then achieve them, this is the highest level of satisfaction that anyone can reach. You set a standard for yourself, you apply yourself, you work hard, you achieve something and you feel satisfied. To be satisfied with your own efforts is the best result of all.

World Records—4 x 200m Freestyle Relay

Kuala Lumpur 1998—7:11.86
Sydney 1999— 7:08.79
Sydney 2000—7:07.65
*Fukuoka 2001—7:04.66

* AT THE TIME OF WRITING, AUSTRALIA STILL HOLDS THIS RECORD

"So you set your goal

Some people set goals by envisaging themselves coming first and beating the others. But, as I said before, you don't actually have control over where you come in a race: there may be someone who is faster than you. You can't change what they've done during their preparation. But you do know what you have done. So you set your goals according to your own abilities, training and preparation. You set goals that are realistic and achievable in the short term—but at the same time, you keep your sights set on the big picture.

World Records—400m Freestyle

Sydney 22 August 1999—3:41.83
Sydney 13 May 2000— 3:41.33
Sydney 16 September 2000—3:40.59
* Fukuoka 22 July 2001—3:40.17

* AT THE TIME OF WRITING, I STILL HOLD THIS RECORD

"I'm addicted to going to the movies. I go every week, and some weeks I go more than once. I love to see everything."

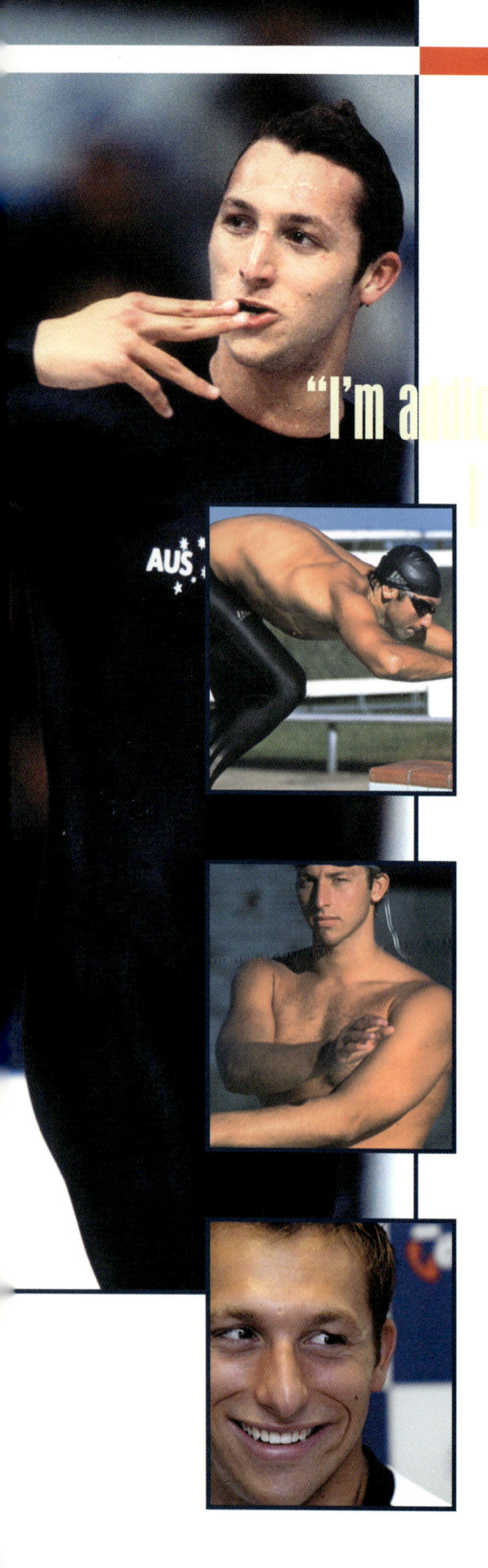

Swimming is only one part of my life. At the moment it plays a major role, but I make sure I do other things as well. I like spending time with my friends, I like shopping and going to the movies. I enjoy all sorts of music—punk, dance, and everything in between. And I still enjoy doing anything where I can express creativity. I think it is important not to let one part of your life take over the rest of it. You need to have a variety of interests to create a balance.

I'm addicted to going to the movies. I go every week, and some weeks I go more than once. I love to see everything. It gives me the chance to forget my own world, and experience someone else's world for a couple of hours. I particularly love horror movies. When I watch movies, I have a tendency to guess ahead, always analysing and trying to work out what's going to happen next.

I usually go out with swimming friends, but sometimes I hang out with old school friends as well. School friends are different from swimming friends, and it's sometimes hard to marry them together. I had a big group of friends at

LIVING YOUR LIFE

school, but the ones I hang out with most are a small group of really close friends that I've known for years. We just do the usual things that everyone does. Hanging out at someone's place, listening to music, going to the beach.

At the moment I'm learning to surf. I can't surf well at all. I started to learn towards the end of 2001, and my goal is to get to the stage where no-one tries to give me advice any more. When I'm out there on the waves, there are experts on all sides telling me to 'do this, do that'. The funny thing is, their advice is always different!

I have grown up in the public eye. Most of the time when I go out, people give me my own space. They turn around and look, and either acknowledge me or my achievements. Because of my public profile, it can sometimes be difficult to do the things I have always done. But I still do them—go shopping, go to the movies, go to the beach.

"At the moment I'm learning to surf. I can't surf well at all."

World Records—200m Freestyle

Sydney 23 August 1999—1:46.34
Sydney 24 August 1999— 1:46.00
Sydney 14 May 2000—1:45.69
Sydney 15 May 2000—1:45.51
Hobart 27 March 2001—1:44.69
* Fukuoka 25 July 2001—1:44.06

* AT THE TIME OF WRITING, I STILL HOLD THIS RECORD

I'm not as well known in parts of Europe and America as I am in Asia and Australia. There are places where everyone recognises me, and other places where no-one does. The thing about being well-known, or famous, is that you can't turn it off. You can't be famous just when you choose to be famous, and then switch it off when you don't feel like it any more. It's constant, one hundred percent of the time. That's the hardest thing. Out on the street, people know who you are and what you're doing all the time.

"There are places where everyone recognises me, and other places where no-one does."

As a kid, I wasn't like some kids who wanted to be famous when they grew up. I wanted to be a good swimmer, and after a while, fame was just something that happened. It's good to remember that famous people are normal, too. You can respect what they have achieved, and appreciate the way they achieved it. But apart from that, all people are basically the same. I've met a few famous people, and I either like them or I don't, just the same as when I meet anyone else.

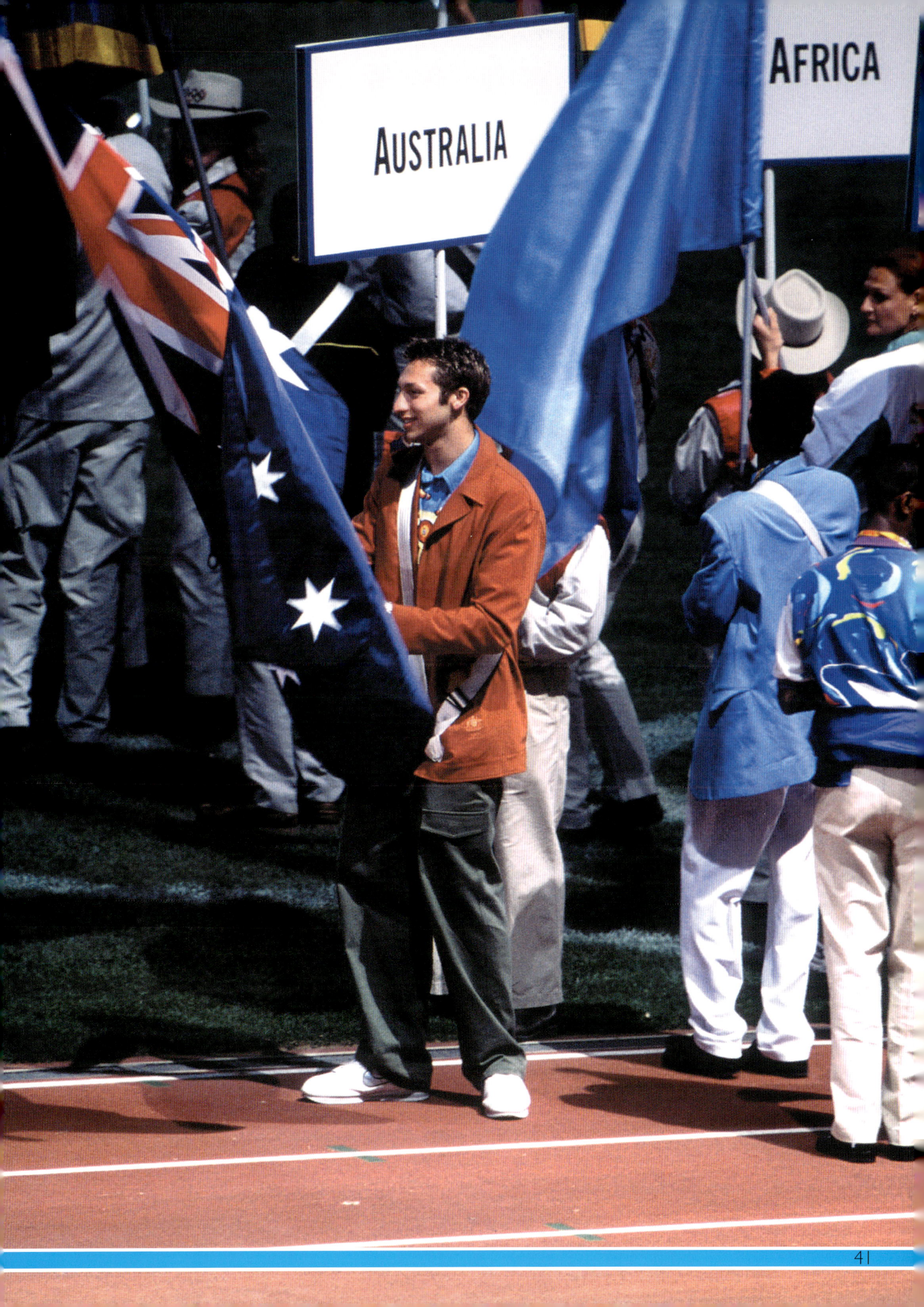
AUSTRALIA
AFRICA

CHARITY

I think that everyone deserves a chance in life: the chance to reach their full potential. And I especially think that children who are ill—and who face greater challenges in life than most of us—should be given as many opportunities as possible.

I appreciate that I've had some great opportunities in my life, more than many other people have had. So, in 2000, I decided I would try to make a positive difference to as many children's lives as I could. To do this, I began a charity called *Ian Thorpe's Fountain for youth*. *Ian Thorpe's Fountain for youth* provides assistance for a number of organisations that support children with illness. These children face great difficulties on a daily basis, due to the treatments and therapies they receive.

I put a lot of time and effort into the Trust, helping young people under the age of twenty. I get more fulfillment out of this work than I get out of most other areas of my life. When I give, I feel rewarded on an emotional level. It is very satisfying to know I have helped someone else, and charity work is an important part of my life.

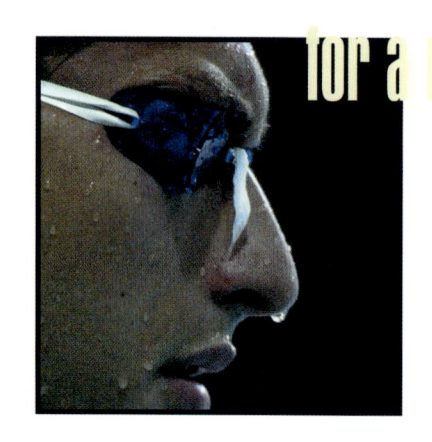

of organisations
that support children with illness."

"My goal is to find something I'll enjoy doing"

LOOKING AHEAD

As far as the future is concerned, I will keep swimming until I stop enjoying it—or else when I know I have reached the point where I am the best swimmer that I can be.

After that, there are many possibilities. My goal is to find something I'll enjoy doing as much as I now enjoy swimming. I've thought of medicine, advertising, architecture, law. It changes every week, just as it did when I was a kid.

I hope I find what it is I want to do. I'm sure it will be something completely away from sport. But I know that whatever it is, I will approach it in just the same way that I have approached my swimming career. I'll set goals, I'll set myself high standards, I'll challenge myself to do my best—and I hope that I'll enjoy it, too!

"As much as I now enjoy swimming, I've thought of medicine, advertising, architecture, law."

World Records held at time of writing

Long Course
3 x Individual World Records
2 x Team World Records

Short Course
1 x Individual World Record
1 x Team World Record

PHOTO CREDITS

Page 1   Photo supplied by adidas.

Page 3   Photos supplied by adidas.

Page 6   Sport the Library/Robb Cox — Telstra Australian Swimming Championships, Brisbane, mens 200m freestyle.

Page 8   (top to bottom)   Photo supplied by adidas.

Sport the Library — Kuala Lumpur 1998 Commonwealth Games, butterfly heats.

Sport the Library/David Madison — Sydney 2000 Olympic Games, 400m freestyle heats. Ian Thorpe, Gold Medal and World Record.

Sport the Library/Jeff Crow — 9th Fina World Swimming Championships, Fukuoka 2001, mens 4 x 100m finals. Australian Team Gold: Geoff Huegill, Matt Welsh, Ian Thorpe, Regan Harrison.

Page 10   Courtesy of Ian Thorpe.

Page 11   Courtesy of Ian Thorpe.

Page 12   Courtesy of Ian Thorpe.

Page 13   Courtesy of Ian Thorpe.

Sport the Library/David Madison — Sydney 2000 Olympic Games, 400m freestyle heats. Ian Thorpe, Gold Medal and World Record.

Page 14   Courtesy of Ian Thorpe.

Page 15   Courtesy of Ian Thorpe.

Page 17   Sport the Library/Ryan Gormly — Sydney 2000 Olympic Games Closing Ceremony. Ian Thorpe Australian Flag Bearer.

Page 18   Sport the Library/Jacki Ames — Sydney 2000 Olympic Games, mens 400m freestyle final. Ian Thorpe, Gold.
Photo supplied by adidas.

Page 19   Sport the Library/Joel Strickland — Ian Thorpe, Telstra Australian Swimmer of the Year 2001.

Page 20   Sport the Library/Robb Cox — 2000 Fina World Cup, Sydney.

Page 22   Sport the Library — Kuala Lumpur 1998 Commonwealth Games, butterfly heats.

(inset) 1. Sport the Library/Jeff Crow; 2. Sport the Library/Ryan Gormly; 3. Sport the Library/Jeff Crow; (strip pic) Sport the Library/Jeff Crow.

Page 23   Photo supplied by adidas.

Page 24   (main pic) Photo supplied by adidas.

(inset) 1. Photo supplied by adidas; 2. Sport the Library/Mark Horsburgh; 3. Photo supplied by adidas.

Page 26   Sport the Library/Tom Putt — Swimmer of the Year Awards, Crown Casino, Melbourne, 2000.

Page 27   (strip pic) Sport the Library/Tom Putt

Page 28   Sport the Library/Robb Cox — Press conference prior to the 2002 Australian Swimming Championships, Brisbane.

Page 29   Sport the Library/Robb Cox — Sydney 2000 Olympic Games, 200m freestyle. Pieter van den Hoogenband, Gold; Ian Thorpe, Silver.

Sport the Library/Robb Cox — Sydney 2000 Olympic Games, mens 4 x 200m freestyle. Ian Thorpe, Gold.

Page 30   Sport the Library/Jeff Crow — 9th Fina World Swimming Championships, Fukuoka 2001, mens 4 x 100m finals. Australian Team, Gold: Geoff Huegill, Matt Welsh, Ian Thorpe, Regan Harrison.

Sport the Library/Jeff Crow — 2001 Telstra Nationals, Hobart, Tasmania, mens 200m heat.

Sport the Library/Darrin Braybrook — 1998 World Swimming Championships, 4 x 200m relay team, Gold: Daniel Kowalski, Ian Thorpe, Grant Hackett, Michael Klim.

Page 31   Sport the Library/Greg Ford — Sydney 2000 Olympic Games, 4 x 100m freestyle relay. Ashley Callus, Chris Fydler, Michael Klim, Ian Thorpe.

Page 32   (strip pic) Sport the Library/Tom Putt — 2001 Goodwill Games, Brisbane. Opening Gala.

(inset) Photo supplied by adidas.

Page 33   Photo supplied by Uncle Tobys.

Sport the Library/Jeff Crow — 9th Fina World Championships, Fukuoka 2001, finals. 6 Gold Medals.

Photo supplied by adidas.

Page 34   Sport the Library/Mark Horsburgh — Sydney 2000 Olympic Games, mens 400m freestyle. Ian Thorpe, Gold.

Photo supplied by adidas.

Page 35   Sport the Library/Robb Cox — Sydney 2000 Olympic Games, mens 4 x 200m freestyle. Australia, Gold.

Page 36   Sport the Library/Jeff Crow — 2001 Telstra Nationals, Hobart, Tasmania, mens 200m heat.

Page 37   Sport the Library/Mark Horsburgh — Sydney 2000 Olympic Games, mens 400m freestyle. Ian Thorpe, Gold.

Sport the Library/Robb Cox

Sport the Library/David Madison

Sport the Library/Scott Grant

Page 38   Sport the Libary/Jacki Ames — Sydney 2000 Olympic Games, mens 400m freestyle final.

Photo supplied by adidas.

Photo supplied by adidas.

Sport the Library/Robb Cox

Page 39   Sport the Library/ Robb Cox — Sydney 2000 Olympic Games, heats. Ian Thorpe, 400m Olympic Record.

Page 40   Sport the Library/Jeff Crow — 9th Fina World Swimming Championships, Fukuoka 2001.

Sport the Library/Jeff Crow — 2001 World Swimming Championships, Fukuoka, Kushida Shrine.

Page 41   Sport the Library/Ryan Gormly — Sydney 2000 Olympic Games Closing Ceremony. Ian Thorpe, Australian Flag Bearer.

Page 42   Sport the Library/Mark Horsburgh

Sport the Library/Mark Horsburgh

Sport the Library/Robb Cox

Page 43   Sport the Library/Robb Cox — 2002 Qantas Skins, Sydney Aquatic Centre, 3 x 100m freestyle.

Photo supplied by adidas.

Page 44   (main pic) as appears in the Autore Magazine, photographed by Troy House.

(inset) as appears in the Autore Magazine, photographed by Troy House.

Page 45   Photos supplied by Omega, photographed by Andrew Gash.

Page 48   Photos supplied by Omega, photographed by Andrew Gash.

47

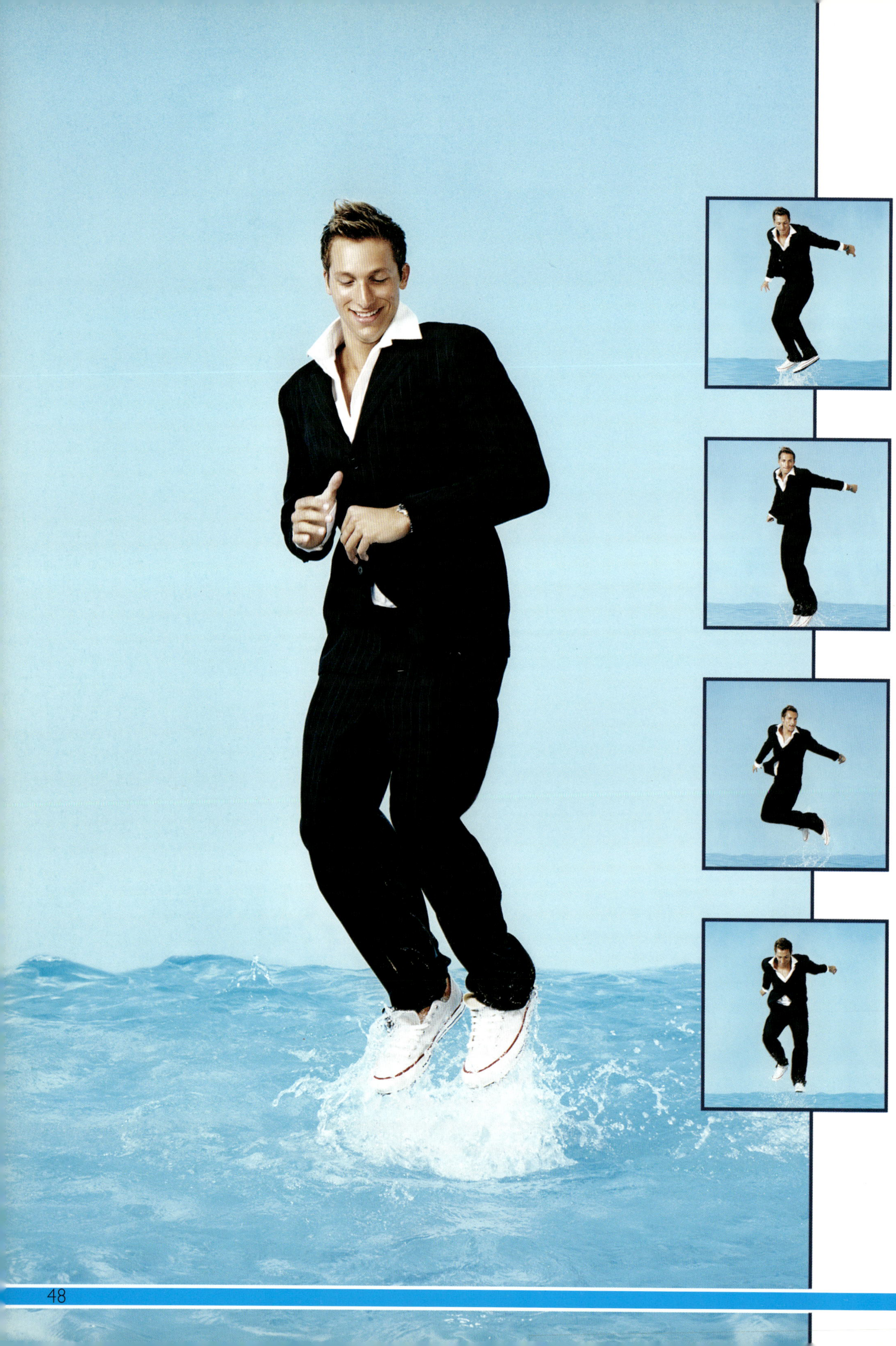